The Christ Life

The Christ Life

by

A. B. Simpson

Christian Publications, Inc.
Harrisburg, Pennsylvania

Christian Publications, Inc.
25 S. 10th Street, P.O. Box 3404
Harrisburg, PA 17105

The mark of *Cp* vibrant faith

Library of Congress Card Number: 80-68837
ISBN: 0-87509-291-8
Printed in the United States of America

Contents

Foreword

The Christ-centered message of Albert B. Simpson, the founder of The Christian and Missionary Alliance is timeless. Breaking through the stereotypes of his day, Simpson preached the gospel with apostolic freshness. He had no time for the niceties of any closed theological system but drew from the wellsprings of the Scripture the truth that Christ is all and in all.

The sum of his doctrinal system was that the believer is in Christ and Christ is in the believer and from that union comes all spiritual reality. *The Christ Life* is one of Simpson's best treatments of this emphasis. The book is uncomplicated and yet profound in its perspective of biblical Christology. Though written in devotional language, it is rich in doctrinal content.

This new edition of *The Christ Life* adds the Scripture references for the reader's convenience.

Introduction

To Dr. A. B. Simpson was granted the privilege of living in a full tide of activity and of ministering through many channels in a measure enjoyed but rarely by the few. For full forty years, with scarcely a day of rest or recreation, he poured out the riches of his spiritual and mental life in a seemingly inexhaustible stream. He was the pastor of a large metropolitan church, which flourished abundantly under his administration. At special services and conventions his messages were in constant demand. As president of a rapidly growing missionary organization, the care of all the churches in a dozen different countries rested chiefly upon his mind and heart. The financial problems incident upon the promotion of a new movement without guaranteed support or any regular sustaining membership was a life task in itself. His busy pen kept the presses of his publishing department in continual operation. About eighty volumes of spiritual teaching were placed at the disposal of the reading public. At least two thousand of his sermons have appeared in print besides numberless tracts and fugitive pamphlets. He composed over a hundred hymns, many of which were widely circulated and not always attributed to their author. Although he was pressed by many duties, his addresses were always finished models of the homiletic art, and like his books, gave evidence of painstaking preparation.

What was the secret of this phenomenally

useful ministry? While recognizing his unusual endowments and the thoroughness of his early preparation, it must be evident that such an unbroken stream of outpoured life can only be explained through acknowledgment of God as the secret spring. Dr. Simpson well illustrated the availability of the promise, "The water that I shall give him shall be in him a well of water springing up into eternal life." In his own experience he illustrated the reality of the Christ life which he has set forth so attractively in this volume. On the fiftieth anniversary of his ordination to the Gospel ministry he returned to a special service in his first charge in Hamilton, Ontario, and there gave the following testimony:

"Fifty years ago the one who addresses you this evening was ordained in this sacred place. He was a young, ambitious minister of twenty-one, and had not yet learned the humbling lessons which God in faithful love is pleased to teach us as fast as we are willing to learn. He was sincere and earnest up to the light that he had received, but even after the nine years of active ministry in Hamilton he had not yet learned the deeper lessons of spiritual life and power which God was pleased to open to him after taking him from this place. There is a remarkable passage in Isaiah telling us that when the Spirit is poured out from on high, the wilderness shall become a fruitful field, and the fruitful field shall be counted for a forest. When that experience came to him, the field of his former ministry, which had been so fruitful, suddenly appeared barren and withered, and he felt that his true ministry had scarcely yet begun.

"I look back with unutterable gratitude to the lonely and sorrowful night when, mistaken in many things, and imperfect in all, not knowing but that it would be death in the most literal sense before the morning light, my heart's full consecration was made. At that time there crossed over the threshold of my being One who was as real to me as He who appeared to John on the isle of Patmos. With unreserved surrender I first could say,

> Jesus, I my cross have taken,
> All to leave and follow Thee;
> Destitute, despised, forsaken,
> Thou from hence my all shall be.

"Never, perhaps, has my heart known quite such a thrill of joy as when the following Sabbath morning I gave out those lines and sang them with all my heart. And if God has been pleased to make my life in any measure a little temple for His indwelling and for His glory, and if He ever shall be pleased to use me in any fuller measure, it has been because of that hour, and it will be still in the measure in which that hour is made the keynote of a consecrated, crucified, and Christ-devoted life."

Of the many hymns which Dr. Simpson has written, the one entitled "Jesus Only" is, perhaps, most typical of His whole testimony. He lived to magnify Christ, and his high ambition was to allow His Lord the fullest opportunity for the expression of His love and power through a crucified and risen human life.

This little volume in the past has shown to many thousands the scriptural pathway that leads to victory and usefulness, and it is now being still more widely distributed in the hope that through it many others shall enter into the enjoyment of "the Christ life."

Walter M. Turnbull

1

Christic the Life

"For the life was manifested, and we have seen it, and declare unto you that eternal life, which was with the Father, and was manifested unto us" (I John 1:2).

"This is the true God, and eternal life" (I John 5:20).

This significant word "LIFE" is the keynote of the two profoundest books in the New Testament, the Gospel of John and the First Epistle of John. The other New Testament books tell of truth, character, and righteousness, but these tell us of life. The others tell the believer what to do and be, but John tells the believer the secret of becoming and accomplishing the things set before him. The mystery of nature is life. The one thing short of which all man's wisdom and resources reach is life. Science can give us the principles of things, and can even reconstruct the forces of nature, but only God can give this strange and subtle thrill which sets all in spontaneous motion, and gives it life.

The Sermon on the Mount tells what an ideal life should be, but the Gospel of John tells how that ideal may become a reality. It starts with the mysterious secret of the New Birth, where life begins, and it leads up to the highest developments of the sanctified and glorified life in the ages to come. The First Epistle of John still more fully unfolds the source, the evolution, and the outflow of divine life.

Before a planet rolled, an insect hummed, or an angel sang, Christ was Himself the eternal life. In the original I John 1:2 is given a stronger emphasis than the Authorized Version expresses, and it reads literally thus: "We show unto you that life, the eternal, which was with the Father and was manifested unto us." I John 5:20 more fully expresses this thought, "This is the true God, and the life eternal." Jesus is the Life, and from Him all life has come. The life of nature is the outflow of His creating power. The life of mind and thought and intellect is but a radiation from His infinite mind. The power that moves the universe from the mightiest sphere to the minutest spray is His personal life, for "By him all things consist," and "In him we live and move and have our being." The tint of the Easter lily, the fragrance of the hyacinth, the teeming life of the vegetable world all come from Him.

Every new-born soul is begotten of His life. The Church of every age and clime is the new creation of His life and power. Every saint is sustained by the life of the living Head. It is so good, therefore, to know that His life is life eternal, and that in Him there is a fountain of life that never can be dry, a sufficiency that never can fail. The word "eternal" here does not merely convey the idea of existence that has neither beginning nor ending, but speaks of a higher sphere of life. It is life that belongs to a loftier plane than the things that are seen and temporal. It is life that is as infinite in its scope as it is enduring in its length, a great unfathomable ocean of boundless fullness and glorious all-sufficiency.

Let us adore the Prince of Life, the Living One,

the Glorious Son of God who stands before us in His radiant and eternal life, proclaiming, "I am he that liveth, and was dead; and, behold, I am alive for evermore. . ." (Rev. 1:18a).

The Life Manifested

"The life was manifested." This includes the whole story of the incarnation and earthly life of the Lord Jesus. This also covers the meaning of the phrase so often used by John in his Gospel and Epistle, "The Word of Life." In the original it says, "The Word of the Life." Just as a word is the expression of a human thought, so He is the expression of God's thought and will, the manifestation of what was already there, but unrevealed. Instead of giving man the written word alone, He sent a living person to exhibit in the actual details of His earthly life the character of God and His purposes of love to the human race.

The story is told of a missionary, who, having failed to bring conviction to the nationals in the Congo by years of preaching, at last stopped in the midst of a course of lessons on the Sermon on the Mount, and announced to the Africans that he was going to live this sermon himself among them. Before the day was over, they gave him ample opportunities of doing so by claiming all his worldly goods, and he, unresistingly, gave "to him that asked, and from him that would borrow turned not away." At nightfall the missionary's wife was in dismay, for her home was stripped, and starvation stared them in the face. But that was only the first act in the drama. Before the night was over, the Africans began to reflect upon the strange example they had witnessed. "This man," they said, "is not like the traders. He does not ask us for things, but he gives us all he has. He must be God's man, and we had better be careful how we treat him." And so the following day witnessed the scene of yesterday reversed and everything brought back with compound interest. This was the second act of the drama. The third act was a great revival, the conversion of a thousand souls, and the organization of the largest church in the Congo. "The life was manifested," and they saw it, and it was an object lesson more mighty than words.

So Christ has manifested in His life the message of the Father and the meaning of the Gospel. His earthly life was a complete pattern of all that God expects a true human life to be. For the first time in the history of the race the Father beheld a man of whom He could say, "In him I am well pleased." Christ's human life covered every side of our earthly relationships that we are called to sustain. The life was manifested in every tint and shade and in every minute detail of typical human experience, so that there is no situation which can arise to which we may not apply the simple watchword, "What would Jesus do?" In our zeal for the great doctrines connected with His death, let us never depreciate the value of His life, and the importance of His perfect example, both as a revelation of God and as an ideal for humanity.

The Life Crucified

While we must not undervalue the life of Christ, we cannot overestimate the significance of His death.

There is a school of teachers who say much about Christian Socialism and the application of Christ's example to the practical details of all our social and secular questions. But these men stop short of Calvary and leave out of view that great event which is the key of all Scripture and all Christian hope and experience. And so very soon in this deeply spiritual epistle, John introduces that expression which bids men pause with a hush of holy awe and tenderness—"The Blood." John had hardly started his letter before two deep crimson shades had covered all the page, the one the dark stain of sin, the other the precious blood of Christ. "The blood of Jesus Christ his Son cleanseth us from all sin" (I John 1:7). This is the great fact back of the cross of Calvary and the resurrection. The death of Jesus Christ, the life so divine, so human, so beautiful, laid down in sacrifice and self-surrender, was not only as an example of submission, teaching us how to die; but a ransom for the guilty and a satisfaction to the righteousness of God for the sins of men. With all his deep insight into the spirit and life of Jesus, John, above all the disciples, recognized the sacrificial meaning of His blood. "Behold the Lamb of God" seems to ring out as the undertone of all his beautiful Gospel. "The blood of Jesus Christ" is the background of his epistles. "Unto him that loved us and washed us from our sins in his own blood" is the keynote of the oft-repeated redemption song of his sublime Apocalypse. The blood of Jesus Christ just means His life, with all its infinite value, given as a substitute and ransom for our forfeited life.

Now it is not enough to appreciate in a sentimental way the sufferings of our Lord, and weep in sympathy over His shame and agony. One may weep over some pathetic story of human sorrow; or under the spell of moving eloquence, and yet know nothing of the power of Christ's blood. The death of Christ stands for a great and potential fact, and is of no value until faith enters into partnership with Him in that fact, and knows by personal appropriation "the fellowship of his sufferings." The death of Christ simply means for me that when He died I died, and in God's view I am now as if I had been executed for my own sin and was now recognized as another person who has risen with Christ and is justified from his former sins because he has been executed for them, "For he that is dead is freed from sin" (Rom. 6:7). Not only so, it is the secret of my sanctification, for on that cross of Calvary, I, the sinful self, was put to death; and when I lay myself over with Him upon that Cross and reckon myself dead, Christ's risen life passes into me and it is no longer my struggling, my goodness, or my badness, but my Lord who lives in me. Therefore while I abide in Him I am counted even as He, and enabled to walk even as He walked.

Beloved, have you entered into the death of Christ and counted it yours, and through it are you now alive unto Him in the "power of his resurrection"?

The Life Risen

It is just as wrong to stop at the Cross as it is to stop before the Cross. It is just as wrong to have merely a dead Christ as to eliminate the death of Christ from our theology. Christ's death is only the background for His resurrection. The life that was laid down was taken up again, and now He stands before us saying, "I am he that liveth, and was dead." It is not the Cross with the Savior hanging on it, but it is the Cross on which He hung, but where He hangs no longer, the grave in which

He lay, but open now, and the very gateway of life immortal. And so this passage is full of suggestions of the risen Lord. "That which our hands have handled of the Word of Life" brings to mind the morning when He stood among them and said, "Handle me and see, for a spirit hath not flesh and bones as ye see me have." There is something infinitely touching in language like this from the pen of John, for he had leaned upon the Master's breast, and doubtless he had proved the reality of his Master's resurrection, and claimed once more the familiar place and touch of love.

And this leads us to notice that this expression, the Blood of Christ, has a higher and deeper meaning in connection with the resurrection, for "the blood is the life," and it is the life of Jesus Christ, His risen life as well as His atoning death, which cleanses us from all sin. We are "saved by his life," quite as truly as by death. In one of the ancient types of Exodus we read of an occasion when Moses, having sacrificed certain bullocks at the foot of the mount and shed their blood upon the altar, took part of the blood in basins and sprinkled it upon the people, and took it up with him into the mount, where they met with God and were accepted because of the blood. The second action of the blood seems to denote the resurrection life of Christ, the life taken back again after it had been once laid down. And so with grateful love we celebrate the victory of our risen Lord and hail Him as the Prince of Life and the Living One, living now as the Conqueror of death, as the Possessor of a new life for all who are united to Him in His death and resurrection.

The Life Indwelling.

For this life is not for Himself, but for us; having risen from the dead He now comes to relive His life in us. This is the secret of sanctification as it is unfolded in the First Epistle of John, and it is the solution of every puzzling problem in connection with that epistle. Perhaps no portion of the New Testament has so many seeming contradictions on the subject of holiness as this epistle. For example, we are told in the first chapter, "If we say that we have no sin, we deceive ourselves, and the truth is not in us" (I John 1:8). And yet a little later we are told with equal emphasis, "Whosoever is born of God doth not commit sin; for his seed remaineth in him: and he cannot sin, because he is born of God" (I John 3:9). Now how can these be reconciled? It is all very simple. First, it is true that we—that is the human "we"—have sin and have sinned. There is no good in us, and we have renounced ourselves as worthless and helpless; but, on the other hand, we have taken Him to be our life, and His life is a sinless one. The seed that He plants is as spotless as that beautiful bulb which, when planted in the unclean soil, grows up as pure as an angel's wing, unstained by the soil around it. It belongs to another element, and is in its own nature essentially and inherently pure.

The key to this whole mystery is supplied by two verses in this epistle. "He that abideth in him sinneth not" (I John 3:6). Here is the secret of holiness, not our holiness, but His. There is no account made here of our perfection, but it is only as we cling to Him and draw our life each moment from Him that we are kept from sin. It is the Indwelling Life.

Again, "We know that whosoever is born of God

18

sinneth not; but he that is begotten of God keepeth himself, and that wicked one toucheth him not" (I John 5:18). Here again the same truth is expressed in a different way. The only Begotten Son of God dwelling in us keeps us from the power of sin and the assaults of Satan; and although the devil often strikes, yet we are like the little insect with the pane of glass between it and the bird of prey, and "that wicked one toucheth us not."

There is one more passage which belongs to this connection. "He that hath the Son of God hath life, and he that hath not the Son of God hath not life" (I John 5:12). Here it is union with the Person of the Lord Jesus that constitutes the source of spiritual life. The secret, therefore, which Paul had found, "Christ in you the Hope of glory," is the secret also of the disciple who leaned on the Master's breast. God grant that we may know, Christ, the secret of life, in all His fullness, the Life Eternal, the Life Manifested, the Life Crucified, the Resurrection Life, the Life Indwelling, through Jesus Christ our Lord, to whom be glory forever and ever. Amen.

2

The Personal Christ

"Abide in me, and I in you. . .for without me ye can do nothing" (John 15:5).

A missionary has stated that the Chinese have learned to differentiate between nominal Christians and true disciples. Every European resident is called a Christian, but they have learned to take those who bear this name on their merits and demerits, and often have good reason to say, "If these drunken, blasphemous foreigners are Christians, then save us from Christianity." But they have found the difference between the true followers of Jesus and mere nominal Christians, and they call the former not Christians but "Jesus people." They have been taught to discriminate between the outward name of Christian and true Christlikeness.

This may serve to illustrate the difference between Christian life and the Christ life. Christian life may be nothing more than the acceptance of certain ideas and principles and the observance of certain forms and rites. Christ life is a vital and divine experience through the union of the soul with the living Christ Himself. Christian life may be an honest attempt to imitate Christ and follow His teachings and commandments, but Christ life is the incarnation of Jesus Himself in your own life. It is the Christ reliving His life in you and enabling you to be and to do what, in your own strength, you never could accomplish.

Personality

The first thing suggested by this thought is personality. The things we value most in the history of the past are not so much the records of events as the revelation of men and women. A country is great not through its magnificent scenery or delightful climate, but because of the men and women that give it its national character. More than our traditions, memories, poetry, literature, and art are our personal heroes. And in our own private life what we value most is not our houses and lands, our commerce and wealth, our culture and progress, but our friends, our loved ones. You would give all the world for one frail little life that is hanging in the balance, and your dearest treasures are the persons you love and call your very own.

And so in the higher realm, the greatest conception in the universe is the conception of the personal God. We rejoice to know that He is not an abstraction or principle, but a living person whom we can touch with our consciousness and embrace with the arms of our faith and love. A lady, just saved from the delusions of Christian Science, exclaimed as she apprehended the personality of Jesus Christ, "How strange that I never realized the awful error they taught me, that Christ was only a principle and not a person. I might as well try to love the grapevine on my trellis as the divine principle. Oh, I am so glad that Jesus is as real as I myself, my own blessed Savior."

The Personal Christ

As we read the story of His life, back of all His wonderful works and words is the Living One

Himself, and so lofty is His personality that even infidelity has been compelled to say that the hardest thing to explain away is not the Bible, but the Christ of the Bible. What other man ever talked so much of Himself or so often used the personal pronoun, and yet it all seems so natural, so becoming, so majestic, and so consistent with His character and personality that we listen with awe and admiration as we hear Him say, "I am the Bread of Life," "I am the Light of the world," "I and my Father are one," "Without me ye can do nothing." We instinctively feel that He has a right to stand without egotism, always in the front of the stage, and that He Himself is greater than all the truths He revealed and all the works He accomplished. And not only so, that personality is still a living Presence. "Lo, I am with you all the days." "Behold, I am alive for evermore." He walks through all the generations as really as in the days of Galilee. He is the Heart as well as the Head of Christianity, "the same yesterday, and today, and forever."

> The healing of His seamless dress
>   Is by our beds of pain;
> We touch Him in life's throng and press,
>   And we are whole again.

> But warm, sweet, tender, even yet,
>   A present help is He,
> And faith has still its Olivet,
>   And love its Galilee.

Salvation through Personal Union with Christ

The personality of Christ is intimately connected with our salvation. We are not saved by embracing a creed or believing a doctrine, but by accepting a Person. "He that hath the Son hath life; and he that hath not the Son of God hath not life" (I John 5:12). "There is therefore now no condemnation to them that are in Christ Jesus. . ." (Rom. 8:1a). Our relation to the Lord Jesus Himself settles our destiny. Jesus Christ is Himself the Father's Gift to sinful men, and the acceptance of that Gift brings us into fellowship with God, and makes us partakers of all the benefits of redemption. Just as Adam was the living personal head of our fallen race, so Christ is the Living Head of the redeemed race, and "For as in Adam all die, even so, in Christ shall all be made alive" (I Cor. 15:22).

Christ Our Life

So also our deeper life is through union with the personal Christ. The apostle has expressed this in the sublime paradox, "I am crucified with Christ: nevertheless I live; yet not I, but Christ liveth in me: and the life which I now live in the flesh I live by the faith of the Son of God, who loved me, and gave himself for me" (Gal. 2:20). Holiness is not personal character slowly attained, but union with the Lord Jesus, so perfect and intimate that He Himself has described it under the figure of the vine and the branches, and adds: "He that abideth in me, and I in him, the same bringeth forth much fruit: for without me ye can do nothing" (John 15:5b). We have not to climb by slow and painful ascent the heights of holiness, but to receive the Holy One Himself to dwell within us and lift us up to all the heights of grace and glory which He Himself has attained. "But of Him are ye in Christ Jesus, who of God is made unto us wisdom, and

23

righteousness, and sanctification, and redemption" (I Cor. 1:30). Our part is not to struggle after ethical culture, but to receive Him, abide in Him, and have Him transfer to us day by day and step by step His own excellence, His own qualities, His own graces, "grace for grace."

Christ Our Physical Life

Our physical quickening comes from the same personal source. The Apostle Paul declares that the life also of Jesus was manifested in his mortal flesh. Paul had his own natural life, but it was limited and often exhausted by the strain of his excessive toils and trials. But he had a second life, "the life also of Jesus," and that enabled him to sustain the pressures for which his own strength was insufficient. The resurrection body of our glorious Lord is the source of physical energy for all His trusting people, and as we abide in Him and draw from Him His sustaining strength, we may "eat his flesh" and "drink his blood," and so "dwell" in Him that it shall be true of us as it was of Him, "Because I live, ye shall live also."

Christ Our Hope

The glorious doctrine of His Second Coming would be nothing without the personal Christ Himself. It is not the reward which He is to bring, or the crown which He is to bestow, which inspires the supreme longing of His followers. But it is the person of the Lord Jesus in that blessed place and time when at last it shall be true, "They shall see his face," and "...the Lamb which is in the midst of the throne shall feed them, and shall lead them unto living fountains of waters" (Rev. 7:17).

The very heart of the advent hope is this, "I will come again, and receive you unto myself; that where I am, there ye may be also" (John 14:3).

Now God has specially qualified His Son to be the sum and substance of the believer's spiritual life. We are told in Colossians 2:9, "For in him dwelleth all the fulness of the Godhead bodily." God has put in Christ everything that man can ever need. He has just concentrated and personified in this blessed Man all His own strength, love, and help, for you and me. In the Vatican at Rome there is a beautifully painted ceiling, so high up that it is impossible to see it; the visitor strains his eye in vain to find it. To meet this difficulty, they have constructed a mirror, so reflecting it that all you have to do is to walk up to a little glass, and there the minutest touches of the fresco in the dizzy heights above are reflected right under your eyes. So He took His glory, and beauty, and help, and put it down on the level of human ignorance and helplessness. He just put it all in the mirror, Jesus Christ, and said, "Is there anything in God you need? There it is in miniature." And then He puts it in your hand, and says, "I have put in Jesus all I am, and now I give Him to you, and you can claim Him for your own."

The Ideal Man

Not only is this blessed Christ the embodiment of God's riches, but He is the pattern and sample of what men ought to be. One Man and only One has lived a perfect human life. With tender pathos God says in one of the prophets: "I looked for a man among all their tribes, and I found none." He looked for someone that could meet the requirements of human character, and found none. But at last there came One, and He looked again, and said with delight, "This is my beloved Son, in whom I am well pleased." "Behold my servant whom I uphold; mine elect, in whom my soul delighteth." He met God's expectation, and became a pattern for all men. So there has lived One on earth who has idealized manhood and womanhood and childhood; the sample of a perfect character, of a woman's heart, of a man's manhood, a pattern for the workman at the bench, for the preacher, for the teacher, for the friend, for the sufferer, for the tempted one—wherever a man may be placed, Jesus has been.

And now this blessed Man is given to you. He says, "Accept Me; not as an example to follow afar off, but as a life to come into you, and impart to you My very nature, and make it second nature to your heart, spontaneous in your choice, victorious in your will, and interwoven with all your emotional life." This is the Christ life. This is the Christ that comes to you today, and offers His personal fullness and all-sufficiency.

In Harmony with Our Nature

A thoughtful, intelligent woman, who was not a Christian, but had a deep hunger for that which is right, posed the question "How can this be so and we not lose our individuality? This will destroy our personality and violate our responsibility as individuals." I said, "Your personality is incomplete without Christ. Christ was made for you, and you were made for Christ, and until you meet Him you are not complete; He needs you as you need Him. Suppose that gas jet should say, 'If I take this fire in, the gas will lose its individuality.' It is only when the fire comes in that the gas fulfills its purpose of being. Suppose the snowflake should say, 'What shall I do? If I drop on the ground, I shall lose my individuality.' But it falls and is absorbed by the soil, and the snowflakes are seen by and by in the primroses and daisies. It is glorious to lose ourselves and rise again in new life in Christ."

Created for Him

It took us days behind a swift engine to cross over the barren plains of the great West. Day by day nothing was seen but sand and sagebrush growing along the track. When I asked about it, I found this was the best soil in the country; where the sagebrush grows, anything will grow. Only one thing was lacking. What was it? Every once in a while we came to an oasis where the grass would be greener than elsewhere; the fruits of the tropics, the fig tree, and the orange groves were growing. What made the difference? As we walked around these farms we found ditches which had caught the mountain stream, and irrigated the land by covering it with water. It needed but one thing to bring it out—water. So you may have all the possibilities, but you come to nothing until you let in the water and become fruitful. The desert needs the water, and the water needs the desert. You need Christ, and Christ needs you. It is this union, this abiding in Him, and He in you, which will bring forth much fruit, for He has said, "without me ye can do nothing."

3

In Christ

"I know a man in Christ" (II Cor. 12:2).

There are two sides from which our union with Christ is presented in the Scriptures; they are best expressed by the Greek preposition "in." It gives us two hemispheres of blessing. The first is, "in Christ"; and the second is, "Christ in you."

They are different thoughts, but each is the complement of the other, and together they constitute the Christ life of which we have been speaking.

First, then, we are represented as in Christ. What is it to be in Christ? It is to be represented by Christ, to have Him stand for us, and enter into all the benefits and privileges of His standing. We are in Adam inasmuch as he is our federal head. We are in our political representatives in the same sense, as they stand for and represent us. And so Christ Jesus is for us, our Representative, and His acts in a measure become ours; He acts for us rather than for Himself.

Our Sins Are Judged

In Christ our sins have been judged. His judgment on the cross was for the sins of His people. He could say in that dark hour, "Now is the judgment of this world." Our sins were on Him, and in Him have been put away, judicially dealt with, visited with the penalty we should have borne, the shame and suffering which we deserved. Entering into union with Him by trusting Him and taking Him for our Savior, saves us from the judgment we deserved. This is the first result of being in Christ, "In whom we have redemption through his blood; the forgiveness of sins, according to the riches of his grace" (Eph. 1:7). "There is therefore now no condemnation to them which are in Christ Jesus" (Rom. 8:1). "He that heareth my word, and believeth on him that sent me, hath everlasting life, and shall not come into condemnation; but is passed from death unto life" (John 5:24).

We Are Justified

Again, if we are in Christ we are justified through His righteousness. Not only have our sins been put away, but our lack of righteousness. He has met the law which we could not obey, and put His own merit and righteousness to our account, and we stand in the same place as though we had kept the law and manifested the same spirit which He manifested without a single flaw. His righteousness passes over to us. It would be possible to justify us from our sins, and leave us, like the poor man just saved out of prison, a wretched, homeless tramp, with nothing on which to start life. Christ not only saves us from the penalty of the law, but gives us His standing. Christ is made unto us righteousness. "For he hath made him to be sin for us, who knew no sin; that we might be made the righteousness of God in him" (II Cor. 5:21). This is the second thing that comes to us by being in Christ; sin cancelled and failure and shortcoming made up by His all-sufficient merit. What joy it inspires!

Jesus, Thy blood and righteousness,
My beauty are, my glorious dress.

If we are in Christ, we are accepted by the Father. Our persons are accepted; we are regarded even as He is regarded, and we enter into the same place He occupies. It is not merely that the judge takes the pen and blots out our sins; not even that the banker takes the pen and writes in his book our infinite credit; but the Father throws His arms around His child, and takes him into Christ's very place.

It is not a millionaire making the tramp rich, but a Father taking the prodigal to His bosom, and making him accepted in "the Son of his love." That is what is meant by being in Christ, sin cancelled, righteousness given and we loved even as He is loved.

Sons of God

If one is in Christ, he enters into His relationships, and becomes to God what Christ is. Jesus said: "My Father, and your Father; my God, and your God." And "as many as received him, to them gave he power to become the sons of God; even to them that believe in his name" (John 1:12). "Ye are all the children of God through faith in Christ Jesus."

Two words are used in the New Testament to describe sonship. One word means a born son. But the other word means much more. The second word for sonship is almost always applied to Christ's sonship, and is rarely used of anybody else but Jesus; but it is also used to denote those who enter into union with Christ. Not only are they born the children of God, but they are accepted in the same sense in which Christ is; that is, they have not only the sonship of the new birth, but the place of Christ Himself. They are not only sons of God, but are "firstborn sons." There is a great difference in the Oriental mind between a son and the firstborn son. The firstborn was the heir; the others came in for something, but the eldest was the heir. So we are told that "He is the firstborn among many brethren"; and believers are called the "firstborn ones." So, beloved, we are children as an angel cannot be; we are children as Jesus is. We are come "to the general assembly and church of the firstborn ones"; We are "heirs of God and joint-heirs with Jesus Christ."

Prayer Answered

In Christ we are presented by our Great High Priest before the throne in our prayers and in our worship, and we are accepted for His sake, even as He Himself is accepted. He hands over the petition in your name, and puts His name on the back; and your prayers go to the Father as if He were asking. He is in His very person and character your Representative. He is not there in His private capacity, and we are not seen in our individual persons, but as one with Christ. And when we come thus, as one with Him, we shall ask what we will and it shall be given. This is the meaning of the promise, "If ye abide in me, and my words abide in you, ye shall ask what ye will, and it shall be done unto you" (John 15:7).

Joint Heirs

We inherit all things in Christ. We sit down with Him on the throne, and all His riches are ours—all things that are to come in the ages of the future. He has linked His future with us; and never again can Christ possess anything without us. Beloved, if you can say, "I am Christ's" you can add, "I have all things in Him." So Paul prays for the Ephesians that they may see what Christ is: "Far above all principality, and power, and might, and dominion, and every name that is named, not only in this world, but also in that which is to come:. . .And gave him to be the head. . .Which is his body, the fullness of him that filleth all in all" (Eph. 1:21-23). He says: "All that is mine is thine." We have begun to enter into the inheritance; and the ages of eternity will not exhaust its ineffable riches.

> All that He has shall be mine,
>   All that He is I shall be;
> Robed in His glory divine
>   I shall be even as He.

4

Christic in Us

Christ in Us

"*And I in you*" (John 15:3).

We pass now to the second thought, "Christ in us." We look up to yonder heaven and see Him there surrounded by all His retinue, endued with all His infinite resources, and enthroned above all power and dominion. Yes; that is all mine; but there is something better. Having seen all the riches of yonder throne, we may bring Him down here, and have Him erect that throne in our heart, and make our heart a very heaven.

Christ in Heaven

If you read the Epistle to the Ephesians you will see that in the first chapter the apostle prays that their eyes may look up into heaven and see what He has. Put the glass to your eye; behold that cloud. See how He ascends; He is above the grave; He is above the fetters of the tomb; He is above the forces of death and hell; He is above the forces of nature; He is above the ranks of angels; He is above all the things that could harm or hurt you. And so he follows Him with the glass of faith, far above all principality, and power, and might, and dominion, and every name that is named, until at last, dazed with the ineffable glory, he pauses overwhelmed.

That is one vision. But if you read further you will see another vision. He has prayed that we might see Christ in heaven. But now he prays that we "may be strengthened with might in the inner man," for something higher and grander. "What is it, Paul? Can there be anything grander?" Oh, yes, there is, and it is this, "That Christ may dwell in your hearts by faith; that ye, being rooted and grounded in love, May be able to comprehend with all saints what is the breadth, and length, and depth, and height; And to know the love of Christ which passeth knowledge, that ye might be filled with all the fullness of God" (Eph. 3:17-19). That is the other heaven, that is the heaven brought down and put into your heart. The first thought is Christ up yonder. This is Christ descending out of heaven like the New Jerusalem, and making His dwelling in your inmost being.

Christ Formed in Us

That was Paul's cry in Galatians 4:19, for his spiritual children in Galatia. "My little children, of whom I travail in birth again until Christ be formed in you." That is his prayer for those who are already Christians. "My little children," you are regenerated; but I am travailing in birth until there shall be something more, even the very person of Christ, born in you! That is more than your being new-born. It is Christ Himself born in the new-born soul. That precious golden casket placed in the believer's breast will open, and in it will come another treasure, brighter than the golden casket; the jewel of Christ's own living presence in his heart of hearts.

"My little children, born you have been, but you want a greater One to come and dwell in you; and I travail in birth, until Christ be formed in you." This is not a character to be formed, but a Person coming to live in us, becoming so one with us that the government shall be on His shoulder, and we shall sing in the empire of the heart, "Unto us a son is given: and the government shall be upon his shoulder: and his name shall be called Wonderful, Counsellor, The mighty God, the everlasting Father, The Prince of Peace. Of the increase of his government and peace there shall be no end" (Isa. 9:6, 7). It is the child Christ born in the heart, so that it becomes not only a converted life, but a Christ life, a divine life. It is not a Christian battling and struggling alone, but a Christian taking into his bosom the Lord to fight his battles, just becoming a temple for God's indwelling; so that the Infinite One can say, "I will dwell in them, and walk in them; and I will be their God, and they shall be my people" (II Cor. 6:16b). It is not, "They shall be my people, and I will be their God," but it is God who is first: He will be their God, and they shall be His people.

Christ's Teachings

The truth of His indwelling is found in all Christ's deeper teachings. He did not venture to give it in the beginning, because His disciples were not ready. He referred to it in the sixth chapter of John, and they were offended when He said: "I am the living bread which came down from heaven; if any man eat of this bread, he shall live for ever: and the bread that I will give is my flesh, which I will give for the life of the world" (John 6:51). They said: "We cannot understand him,"

"This is an hard saying," and went away and walked with Him no more. They thought it transcendental and sentimental.

In the fourteenth and fifteenth chapters of John He unfolds this truth once more. He says: "He that hath my commandments, and keepeth them, he it is that loveth me: and he that loveth me shall be loved of my Father, and I will love him, and will manifest myself to him. Jesus answered and said unto him, If a man love me, he will keep my words: and my Father will love him, and we will come unto him, and make our abode with him" (John 14:21, 23). And again, in the fifteenth chapter: "I am the vine; ye are the branches: He that abideth in me, and I in him, the same bringeth forth much fruit; for without me ye can do nothing. . . .If ye abide in me, and my words abide in you, ye shall ask what ye will and it shall be done unto you" (John 15:5, 7). And again He says: "The Holy Ghost, whom the Father will send in my name, he shall teach you all things, and bring all things to your remembrance, whatsoever I have said unto you" (John 14:26). In the seventeenth chapter of John He says: "O righteous Father, I pray for them, that they may be one, as we are one. Thou in me, and I in them." And He adds: "That the love wherewith thou has loved me may be in them, and I in them."

This was the last prayer Christ ever offered for His people: "I in them." That seventeenth chapter of John was the highest utterance of Christ in this world; and these last three words, "I in them," are most precious of all. Oh, if we want His prayer fulfilled, we must enter into the meaning of this message, and never stop short of its actual experience.

Again and again, throughout the latter epistles, we find this same truth repeated. In Colossians the apostle speaks of "The secret or mystery which has been hid for ages, but is now made manifest." He seems almost afraid to state it. Like someone about to tell good news, he hesitates; it is so overwhelming. That mystery hidden for ages past is now to be manifested to those who believe. This truth is like the white stone with the name upon it "which no man knoweth saving he that receiveth it" (Rev. 2:17b). Paul has at last been permitted to give the bride this signet ring. This is the secret: "Christ in You the Hope of Glory." Have you received it? Has it been opened to you? It is the sapphire jewel that will outflash the glories of the New Jerusalem.

Paul testifies in Galatians 2:20, "I am crucified with Christ: nevertheless I live; yet not I, but Christ liveth in me: and the life which I now live in the flesh I live by the faith of the Son of God, who loved me, and gave himself for me." That is the way Paul obtained it, by dying to his own life and taking Christ instead.

The Lord came to the isle of Patmos, and gave John this message: "Behold, I stand at the door, and knock: if any man will hear my voice, and open the door, I will come in to him, and sup with him, and he with me" (Rev. 3:20). It was written to the Church of Laodicea—the people that called themselves the Church of God, but whose hearts were closed; self was on the throne. "I am rich," they said, "and increased with goods, and have need of nothing." Outside stood the pleading form of Jesus, His locks wet with the dew of the morning. Christ Himself was knocking and waiting and saying: "If any man will hear my voice, and open the door, I will come in to him, and sup with him, and he with me." Oh, is it not a pathetic picture, a shameful picture! This message was addressed to the last of the seven Churches, the closing representative of modern Christianity; the Church of today. He was outside the door, and the Church inside, satisfied to have Him there. And He is saying: "Thou knowest not that thou art wretched, and miserable, and poor, and blind, and naked"; while they said, "I am rich and increased with goods, and have need of nothing."

Christ's Own Dependence

Christ said in the fifth chapter of John, that He had no independent life of His own, but was constantly dependent on His Father for every word and act. The Christ life is the very life that Christ lived on this earth. Is it not strange to hear Him say, with all His resources, "I can of mine own self do nothing: as I hear, I judge . . ." (John 5:30). Jesus, who walked this earth as our Example, never tried to be independent, but He constantly received His Father's life; drew His being from His Father, and lived by Him. "As the living Father has sent me, and I live by the Father, so he that eateth me, even he shall live by me."

So He wants you and me to live by Him. He is just repeating the life He lived when He trod the hills of Galilee; utterly dependent, an empty vessel, receiving all from above. So, now, He requires you and me to be empty vessels, receiving all from Him. "In that day"—"When the Spirit of Truth is come," will He bring something that will make you important, something that will make you so pure that you will sit down and look at your holiness? Not a bit of it. This is what happens when the Holy Spirit comes into the heart: "At that day ye shall know that I am in the Father." You shall understand how I have been linked with Father and dependent on Him for My very life. And ye shall learn thus to depend upon Me. "At that day ye shall know that I am in my Father, and ye in me, and I in you" (John 14:20). You will not know that you are holy and strong; but you will know that I am holy and strong, and in you as your purity and strength.

He represents this union by the double figure of a glorious sunrise, and a home scene. First, "I will manifest myself" (John 14:21). This is a Greek word, meaning to shine forth, conveying the same idea as Isaiah when he says: "Arise, shine; for thy light is come, and the glory of the Lord is risen upon thee." This is what Jesus means when He says: "I will manifest myself to him." How it suggests the closing promise of the Old Testament: "But unto you that fear my name shall the Sun of righteousness arise with healing in his wings;. . ." (Mal. 4:2a).

The other figure is that of the home. "We will come unto him, and make our abode with him" (John 14:23). He will make our spirits His dwelling place. The once sad and sinful heart now indwelt by Christ shall become the palace of a king, where the believer shall dwell under the shadow of His presence, and in the joy of His fellowship.

> Christ never is so distant from us
>   As even to be near,
> He dwells within the yielded spirit,
>   And makes our heaven here.

5

How to Enter In

"Lord, how is it that thou wilt manifest thyself to us and not unto the world?" (John 14:22).

But how does He thus manifest Himself as He does not unto the world? First, He Himself brings us into this state. He does not leave us to climb up to it alone. He does not build a palace yonder and say, "If you can reach it, it will be a blessed place," but He brings us right up to the palace.

John Bunyan, when God came to him with conviction of sin, saw in vision a house of beauty and of blessing, where holy men and women were singing together in the very light of the Lord. But he was outside and could not get within. It seemed that a barrier of rocks arose between them and him. He saw how happy those people were, and how bright the scene, and how real the joy. But he was out in the dark and cold. And that is the way it seems to some. They say: "It is beautiful to live a life like that, where it is constant rest and victory, and where our troubles do not drown us; where the great whirlpool of sin does not draw us in, and we have Christ to bless us and to make us a blessing to others, but it is not possible for us to get there."

I remember a meeting where a good man got up and told the people what Christ would do for them if they would only let Him in to do it. "But," he said, "you must be prepared for it. You must get cleansed first, or Christ will not come." I saw those countenances go down and the people seemed to be asking by their looks: "Oh, dear, how shall we get cleansed?" And I longed to say, Beloved, the cleansing is just what Christ Himself waits to give you."

Christ Our Holiness

To get a holiness of our own, and then have Christ reward us for it, is not His teaching. Christ Himself is our holiness; He will bring His own holiness, and come and dwell in our hearts forever.

People sometimes used to fix up the shanties on the vacant lots in the upper part of New York City, where many poor people lived. The wash woman would spend a few dollars to clean up her shanty and whitewash its walls, and would feel that she had made it look respectable. But when a millionaire purchased that lot, he did not fix up that old shanty, but tore it down, and built a mansion in its place.

It is not fixing up the house that we need. Give Christ the vacant lot, and He will excavate below the old life and build a worthier house, where He will live forever. Christ must be the preparation for the blessing as well as the blessing. It is as when a great Assyrian king used to set out on a march. He did not command the people to make a road, but he sent on his own men, and they cut down the trees, and filled the broken places, and leveled the mountains. So Christ will work in us if we let Him be the coming King and the Author and Finisher of our faith.

Our Death to Self

A lady once told me that Christ had said to her,

"I will be thy death, and I will then be thy life." Do not try to be your death. Take Christ for the crucifixion. Christ will completely undertake and finish the work of uprooting, casting away, and crucifying. One does not need to stand in the dissecting room working over his spiritual corpse, or trembling with the knife of the suicide, trying to stab himself to death. Be done with all that torture. Trust Him to be the power to slay self. Hand self over to Christ and say, "Here is the culprit, Lord; I deliver him over to you. I cannot slay him, but I want him killed. I want you to still these throbbing pulses of passion, and let peace come instead. I cannot do it. But I give Thee the right to slay me in Thine own way, and here once and forevermore I yield myself to Thee."

Our Life and Purity

Christ will not only be the death of self, and the power to put old self aside, by His Spirit and grace, but He will be in us the new life of purity and power. He will cleanse us, and let us share His life. And there will be such a sense of its being a life that does not belong to you. When one receives Christ there is no pride because of one's own goodness; but we feel like lying in the dust and saying, "I am nothing but the chief of sinners." But at the same time, he is conscious that a blessed stream of purity is flowing through every avenue of his being. When temptation comes He meets it by the blessed supply of His Spirit, and one is lifted above it; the positive destroys the negative; the heavenly repels the earthly and the evil.

It as when, on a sultry summer day, suddenly the refreshing showers fall, and in a few moments everything is cleansed and purified. The grass is fresh and green. The flowers lift up their heads with beauty and brightness. The air is full of life, and the sweet fragrance of nature fills the senses. So it is when the Spirit of Christ comes to refresh the weary, sinful heart. His presence will be like those showers, dropping upon the spirit and cleansing it from the very dust of the defiling earth, or like the pebble by the stream, kept clean in its ceaseless flow.

Our Peace

Again, He is not only our death and our life, but He becomes our peace. You read much of this in the Gospels. "My peace I give unto you. Let not you heart be troubled, neither let it be afraid." Tranquility is one of the chief features of this life of Christ within. The natural turbulence and irritation will be stilled. One shall be self-poised, or, rather, Christ-poised, and there will be a sense of calm, strength, and rest. Instead of storming through life, the believer will be divinely quiet. Down in the depths of life there shall be a consciousness of "the peace of God that passeth all understanding, keeping the heart and mind through Christ." Christ comes into the inner chambers of the heart, and although there may be turbulence and tribulation outside, whispers, "These things I have spoken unto you, that in me ye might have peace. In the world ye shall have tribulation: but be of good cheer; I have overcome the world" (John 16:33).

Our Joy

This indwelling Christ is more than peace—He is also joy. "That my joy might remain in you, and that your joy might be full" (John 15:11). Zephaniah had laid hold of this thought, "The Lord thy God in the midst of thee is mighty; he will save, he will rejoice over with thee with joy; he will rest in his love, he will joy over thee with singing" (Zeph. 3:17). Sometimes He will be silent in His love. He will sometimes hold the tides of joy so calm and still that one will be afraid to stir for fear of breaking the spell. And then at other times the joy will sweep through all the channels of his being. Alternately He will rest and then break out in transports of joy.

The peace is abiding; the joy is occasional. When there is need to rise above some earthly trial, then the fountains overflow. So He came to Paul and Silas when their bones were aching, and they were sore from the stripes of the inner prison. They could not keep it back. They sang for joy. It came when the people of Antioch had chased them out of the city, and "the disciples were filled with joy and the Holy Ghost." It came to the martyrs when they were roasting at slow fires, and they turned to their persecutors and said, "We do not feel the flames, the joy is so great; it fills our being and quenches the pain." It was the Spirit of Him who, on the eve of the Cross, turned from His own troubles, began to comfort them, and said, "Let not your heart be troubled."

Christ in us will be our faith. We will be able to say, "The life I now live I live by the faith of the Son of God." When you have this faith it will be second nature to believe God. You will be conscious of a supernatural faith, and you will not be trying to have faith, but simply responding to His call, "Have the faith of God."

Our Love

Again, the love of God will be shed abroad in your hearts; not the love of your natural heart, but the love of God. If Christ is in you, you will be conscious of a divine love for Christ, and know that it is not your love but His. And you will have new affections and friendships to all men, loving in and for Him only.

Our Wisdom

If we have this indwelling Christ, He will be our wisdom. He will in some way touch our very thoughts. He will give us new conceptions of truth. You will have His intuitions about the things you ought or ought not to do, yet all in perfect harmony with our nature, so blended with the faculties He has given us, that the thoughts and impulses will seem to be our own.

Our Power

He will be the strength of God in you. Paul said, "...I also labor, striving according to his working, which worketh in me mightily" (Col. 1:29). So it will not be our doing, but Christ enabling us, Christ giving us His power to work for others, and for the effectual building up of His kingdom. So that, while we are a weak woman, or an imperfectly educated man, we will be filled with the consciousness, "I am speaking in the strength of God," and we will know that the Word of God shall not return to Him void.

It is blessed to work and speak and pray in the power of Christ. And it is mockery and worse than vain to attempt it without. Christ will be our

45

power: "All power is given unto me in heaven and in earth. . ." (Matt. 28:18b), ". . .and, lo, I am with you alway. . ." (Matt. 28:20b).

Our Prayer

Christ in us will be our prayer life. He will intercede within us. And there will be sometimes the groans and tears of His own Gethsemane, and again the effectual prayer that claims all things in His name.

Our Praise

He will be our praise as well as our prayer. He will come to the heart after it has presented its petition, and touch it with the voice of thanksgiving, enabling us to bless God for the answer that is coming.

Our Health

If Christ is in our heart, He will be our physical strength and life. He will inspire our vital functions with energy, and make us know that the life also of Jesus is being manifested in our mortal body.

Our Patience

When Christ is in us, He is our patience. One part of Christ's life was suffering; so a large part of ours will be suffering with Him. That cross will also rest upon the Mount Calvary of the believer's life, and he will gladly share it with Him; not suffering needlessly, not suffering to please the enemy. It is suffering in order that a cup of cold water might be given to another or to help carry a burden, or bear them through places where they would sink. This is helping Christ bear His heavy load for the suffering hearts of the world. When suffering comes, as it came to Him, from opposing men and devils, then He will enable us to become more than conquerors.

How to Enter In

When I was in Scotland I went to visit an old cemetery in the city of Sterling and as I gazed upon one grey monument, looking back through the mist of years, it brought to my mind the story of the Covenanters. It was the monument of Margaret Wilson. It told how that dear young saint, a girl in her teens, held so to her love of Jesus that the pleadings of father and mother and friends kept her not back from death. "Only one little word, Margaret, one little word, and your life will be spared," they said. "I canna speak the word that shall dishonor Jesus," she replied. "Remember your father's grief," he begged the night before she died. She stroked his grey hairs, and said, "I canna speak the words you bid me speak."

Next morning they took her out, those rude, hard men, and tied her to the stake and put it in the sea. And they tied to another a grey-haired old saint, and they put her a little farther out in the wild sea so that Margaret Wilson could first see her die. And they said, "Margaret Wilson, don't you see her agony? Won't you now recant?" And she said, "No, I do not see her; I only see Jesus in His suffering servant wrestling there." And a little later the chariot of the Lord was waiting to bear her conquering spirit home.

That is our watchword, "Christ in one of His

members suffering there." "Not I, but Christ." Thus we can overcome; thus we can live; thus we can suffer. Believers can be "more than conquerors through him."

Our Will

If Christ be thus in us, He will be in the very center of our being—our will. This is the helm of character. But Christ will take the will and bend it until it shall be no longer stubborn. He will make it yield to His will and choose what He chooses. He will make it delightfully spontaneous. When I was a lad I made my own sled runners, and they would always break. But one day a carpenter showed me a better way to make runners. He put it in the steam boiler, and then it would bend easily.

Christ does not want to break our will, but put it in the fire of His love, and work in us to will and to do of His good pleasure. And then He will take it and make it strong. When the sled runner was bent, the carpenter showed me how to make it so firm that it would not spring back again. So Christ can make our will firm.

6

How to Abide

"And now, little children, abide in him; that, when he shall appear, we may have confidence, and not be ashamed before him at his coming" (I John 2:28).

It would seem as though John meant that only little children could abide in Him; that only when we get to be little can we know the Lord in His fullness; only when we cease from manly or womanly strength and become dependent can we know His strength as our support and stay. John counted himself among the little children, because he says, "we" when he addresses us. He was indeed a little child in spirit from the time Boanerges died, and John laid his head on Jesus' breast to be strong no more in himself, and to be seen no more apart from the enfolding arms of Jesus.

We have seen Christ in His personal glory; we have seen what it is to be in Him and to have Him in us, and now we want to have these impressions stereotyped. John says, "Little children, abide in him, that when he shall appear we may have confidence."

How may we, the believer, maintain this abiding life? You have surrendered; you have given up your strength as well as your will; you have consented that henceforth He shall support your life. Like a true bride, you have given up your very person, your name, your independence, so that now He is to be your Lord. Your very life is merged in Him, and He becomes your Head and your All in All. Now, beloved, how is this to be maintained? He says we are to abide, and He will abide in some sense according to our abiding. "Abide in me, and I in you."

Live by the Moment

First, it must be a momentary life, not a current that flows on through its own momentum; but a succession of little acts and habits. You have Him for the moment, and you have Him perfectly; you are perfectly saved this moment; you are victorious this moment, and that which fills this moment is large enough to fill the next, so that if you shall renew this fellowship every moment, you shall always abide in Him. Have you learned this? The failures in your life mostly come through lost moments, broken stitches, little interstices, cleavages in the rock where the drops of water trickle down and become a torrent. But if you lose no steps and no victories, you shall abide in constant triumph.

First, then, learn this secret, that you are not sanctified for all time so that there will be no more need for grace and victory; but you have grace for this moment, and the next moment, and by the time life is spent, you shall have had a whole ocean of His grace. It may be a very little trickling stream at first; but let it flow through every moment, and it shall become a boundless ocean before its course is done.

Definite Acts of Will

Next, this abiding must be established by a succession of definite acts of will, and of real, fixed, steadfast trust in Christ. It does not come as a spontaneous and irresistible impulse that carries you whether you will or not, but you have to begin by an act of trust, and you must repeat it until it becomes a habit. It is very important to realize this.

A great many think, when they get a blessing, that it ought to sweep them on without further effort. It is not so. An act of will, an act of choice is the real helm of spiritual life. One is saved from sin by actually choosing Jesus as his Savior; he is consecrated by definitely giving up himself and taking Christ for everything.

So beloved, we must keep the helm fixed, and press on, moment by moment, still choosing to trust Christ and live by Him until at last it comes to be as natural as breathing. It is like a man rescued from drowning; when they take him from the water, respiration seems to be stopped. And when it returns, it is not spontaneous, but a succession of labored pumpings; they breathe the air in and they breathe the air out, perhaps for half an hour; then an involuntary action is noticed, and nature comes and makes the act spontaneous; and soon the man is breathing without effort.

But it came by a definite effort at first, and by and by it became spontaneous. So with Christ: if one would have this abiding in Him become spontaneous, he must make it a spiritual habit. The prophet speaks of the mind "stayed on God," and David says, "My heart is fixed, trusting in the Lord." We begin by determining, and we obey Him no matter what it costs; and by and by the habit is established.

The Law of Habit

Then comes the third principle: habit. Every

habit grows out of a succession of little acts. No habit comes full-grown into your life; it grows like the roots of a tree, like the fibers of the flesh, as the morsels of food are absorbed into your body. When a man goes steadily along in a course of life, it is likely that that course was established by the habit of years. The stenographer takes down words as fast as they are spoken. At first it is clumsy and slow work; but at length it becomes a habit, and now the stenographer does not have to stop and think how to make the characters; they come as naturally as words come to the lips. So it is with writing: we remember how painfully at first we had to hold the pen, but now dash off our signature, and it is always the same; our friends know it, our banker knows it; and it can be identified as ours. How did it come about? Because for years we have made the same marks. This is the reason, beloved, that it pays to plod; the habit becomes at length a necessity, and is easier as it grows.

It is so with evil; it is easier for a man to go down the longer he goes down, and it is easier for him to go up the longer he goes up. And so it is with looking to Jesus; it is like the movement of the eye—the lid moves instinctively and the Bible uses it as a figure of God's care. "Keep me as the apple of thine eye." Before the dust can hurt the eye, the little curtain falls over the tender eyeball. So one finds himself instinctively holding his tongue when he would have felt like talking. So he learns to discern the very scent of evil before it comes and inarticulately breathe a prayer to heaven before the danger reaches him. Thus also will the habit of obedience be formed; it comes by doing steadily, persistently, and faithfully what the Lord would have us to do. He is putting us to school in these little trials, until He gets the habit confirmed, and obedience becomes easy and natural.

Self-Repression

Again, if we would abide in Christ we must continually study to have no confidence in self. Self-repression must be ever the prime necessity of divine fullness and efficiency. How quickly one springs up in self-assertion when any emergency arises. He knows how easy it was for Peter to step forth with his sword drawn before he knew whether he was able to meet the foe or not. That which is done in sudden impulse, can result in weeks of regret. Take the Lord instead of impulse. It is only as we get out of the way of the Lord that He can use us.

And so, beloved, let us practice the repression of self and the suspending of our will about everything until we have looked to Him and said, "Lord, what is Thy will? What is Thy thought about it?" When you have that, you and He are not at cross-purposes; and there is blessed harmony. Those who thus abide in Christ have the habit of reserve and quiet; they are not reckless talkers; they will not always have an opinion about everything, and they will not always know what they are going to do. They will be found holding back rash judgments, and walking softly with God. It is the headstrong, impulsive spirit that keeps one from hearing and following the Lord.

Dependence

If we would abide in Christ we must remember that Christ has undertaken not only the emergencies of life, but everything; and so we must cultivate the habit of constant dependence on Him; falling back on Him and finding Him everywhere; recognizing that He has undertaken the business of our life, and there is not a difficulty that comes up, but He will carry us through if we let Him have His way, and just trust Him.

Recognizing His Presence

Again, if you would abide in Christ you must cultivate the habit of always recognizing Him as near, in your heart of hearts, so that you need not try to find Him, reaching out to the distant heavens and wondering where He has gone. He is right here; His throne is in your heart; His resources are at hand. There may be no sense of God's presence, but just accept the fact that the Spirit is in your heart, and act accordingly. Bring everything to Him, and soon the consciousness will become real and delightful. Do not begin with feeling—begin with acting as though He were here. So, if you would abide in Christ, treat Him as if He were in you, and you in Him; and He will respond to your trust, and honor your confidence.

God in Everything

To abide in Christ is to recognize that Christ is in everything that comes in life; and that everything that occurs in the course of Providence is in some sense connected with the will of God. That trying circumstance was not chance, something with which Christ had nothing to do, and which we can only protest and wonder how God can let such things be. We must believe that God led in it, and though the floods have lifted up their heads on high, yet God sits on the throne, and is mightier than the great sea billows and the noise of many waters. We must believe that He will "cause the wrath of man to praise him, and the remainder thereof will he restrain." We must say: "God is our refuge and strength, a very present help in trouble. Therefore will not we fear, though the earth be removed, and though the mountains be carried into the midst of the sea; Though the waters thereof roar and be troubled, though the mountains shake with the swelling thereof" (Ps. 46:1-3).

Everything need not be regarded as the very best that one would choose, or the very best that God will ultimately bring about. It is allowed, either that God may show us His power to overcome it, or may teach us some lesson of holiness, trust, tranquility, or courage. It is something that, under the circumstances, fits into God's purposes; and, therefore, we are not to look for different circumstances, but to conquer in these already around us. We are not to run away and say, "I will abide in Christ when I get to where I want to be," but we must abide in Christ in the ship and the storm, as well as in the harbor of blessing. Recognize that everything is permitted by God, and that He is able to make all things work together; and not only so, but to make us know they are all for our good, and they are working out His purposes.

Watch the Outward Senses

Abiding in Christ requires being very watchful of the senses. Nothing so easily sets us wandering out into dangerous fields and by-path meadows as the senses of the body. How often our eyes will take us away! Walking down the street one finds a thousand things to call him from a ate of recollection. Some people's eyes are like a spider's—they see behind and before and on every side. Solomon says, "Let thine eyes look right on, and let thine eyelids look straight before thee." Letting the world in, no matter by what door it comes, separates us from the presence of our Lord.

If we listen to one-hundredth part of the conversation even of Christians we will be thoroughly defiled; and so you have to hold your ears, and your eyes, and live in a little circle. One ought not to manage half so many things as he undertakes. This causes anxiety.

There is a little creature called the water spider, and it lives in the water, away down in the mud lake of the marsh. It just goes down a few inches, and lives there all the time. It has a strange apparatus by which it is able to gather around itself a bubble of air a few times larger than its body. It goes to the surface and fills it with air and goes down, and this little air bubble forms an atmosphere for it, and there it builds its nest and rears its young. Because of the principle that where the air is the water cannot enter, that spider is as safe in its little home with the dark water all around it, as it would be if it lived above in the clear air. So we can get into our element and stay there with Him, and although there is sin around us, and hell beneath us, and men are struggling and tempted and sinning, we shall be as safe as the saints above, in the heavenlies, in Christ Jesus.

Internal Prayer

Once more, if we would abide in Him, we must cultivate the habit of internal prayer, communing with God in the heart. We must know the meaning

56

of such words as "God is a Spirit, and they that worship him must worship him in spirit and in truth." "In everything give thanks, for this is the will of God concerning you." This habit of silent prayer, not in words, but in thought, is one of the secrets of abiding. There is an old word the mystics used—"recollection." It might be called a recollected spirit.

Vigilance

There is another word in connection with abiding: it is vigilance—being wide-awake. It is the opposite of drifting. It is the spirit of holding, and being ever on guard, and yet sweetly held by the Lord. Now this does not mean that you have to do all the holding and watching; you are to have your hand on the helm, and Christ will do the steering. It is like the brakes on the train—the brakeman only touches the lever and sets the current in motion; the engineer does not have to make the train go, he has only to turn the throttle. The Christian does not need to fight his battles. He has only to give the watchword, and the powers of heaven follow it up if it is in the name of Jesus. So one may ever abide in fellowship and victory moment by moment, until at last Christ becomes the atmosphere of his very life.

Let God Lead

If we would abide in Christ, we must stop trying to have God help us, and fall into God's way and let Him lead. The believer must rid himself of the idea that he has chosen to serve Christ and Christ must help him. Rather, he has come into Christ's way and He is carrying him because He cannot go any other way. If one gets on the bosom of the river, one has to go down the river; if one is in the bosom of God, one has to go with Him. When the life is surrendered to God, it will be as strong as omnipotence and as sweet as heaven.

The Unexpected

Perhaps, it is well to speak of the unexpected that may come. Sometimes the Lord lets sudden temptations sweep over us to put us on guard. When such things come into the life, take them as from Him, sent to put us on the alert—like the falling of an eyelash lets the eye know it is being threatened. These temptations spring often from our own heedlessness. When one is getting out of the way, the Lord permits the trial to let him know that he had been in the enemy's country. If we abide in Him, all evil will have to strike us through Him. Perhaps we were a little out of center and Christ let the enemy come to frighten us back to Him, just as the shepherd's dogs are sent to drive the lambs into the fold. A little fall is better than ultimately to meet with disaster.

Failures

But if, notwithstanding all his care, one makes a mistake, he should not despair. He should not say, "I have lost my blessing." "I have found this life impracticable"; but remember that "if we confess our sins, he is faithful and just to forgive us our sins, and to cleanse us from all unrighteousness."

How to Make God Real

God is not real to many people. He does not seem

so real to that man as his difficult task; He does not seem so real to that woman as her work and her trials; He does not seem so real to that sufferer as his sickness. How shall we make Him real? The best way I know is to take Him into the things that are real. That headache is real. Take Him into it, and He will be as real as the headache, and a good deal more, for He will be there when the headache is gone. That trial is real; it has burned itself into your life; God will be more so. That washing and ironing are real; take God into your home, and He will be as real. Christ is real when we link Him with our life.

So the banyan tree grows. First, its trunk and branches shoot up to heaven, and then the branches grow down into the ground and become rooted in the earth, and by and by there are a hundred branches interwoven and interlaced from the ground so that the storm and the winds cannot disturb it, and even the simoon of the Indian Ocean cannot tear it up. It is rooted and bound together by hundreds of interlacing roots and branches. And so when God saves a soul He plants one branch; but when He comes to fill and sanctify and help in your difficulties, each is another branch; and thus your life becomes rooted and bound to God by a hundred fibres, and all the power of hell cannot break that fellowship or separate you from His love.

> Lord Jesus, make Thyself to me
> A living, bright reality,
> More present to faith's vision keen
> Than any outward object seen,
> More dear, more intimately nigh,
> Than e'en the sweetest earthly tie.

Nearer and nearer still to me
Thou living, loving Saviour be.
Brighter the vision of Thy face,
More glorious still Thy words of grace;
Till life shall be transformed to love,
A heaven below, a heaven above.

7

Through Death to Life

"If any man will come after me, let him deny himself, and take up his cross, and follow me" (Matt. 16:24).

Here lies the great difference between the world's gospel and the Lord's gospel. The world says, when it bids you good-bye, "Take care of yourself." The Lord says, "Let yourself go and take care of others and the glory of your God." The world says, "Have a good time, look out for number one." But the world gets left in the end, and the last comes in first. The man that lets go gets all, and the man who holds fast loses what he has, and the Lord's words come true—"Whosoever will save his life shall lose it, and whosoever will lose his life for my sake shall find it."

So the law of sacrifice is the greatest law in earth and heaven. The law of sacrifice is God's great law. It is written in earth and every department of nature. We tread on the skeletons of ten thousand millions of generations that have lived and died that we might live. The very heart of the earth itself is the wreck of ages and the buried life of former generations. All nature dies and lives again, and each new development is a higher and larger life built on the wrecks of the former. A corn of wheat must fall into the ground and die, or else be a shriveled-up seed, but as it dies it lives and multiplies, and grows into the beautiful spring, the golden autumn, and the multiplied sheaves. And so it is in the deeper life of the higher world, as you rise from the natural to the spiritual. Everything that is selfish is limited by its selfishness. The river that ceases to run becomes a stagnant pool, but as it flows it grows fresher, richer, fuller.

If we turn our natural eye upon self, we cannot see anything. It is as we look out that the vision of the world bursts upon us. The very law of the natural life is love for others, caring for others by giving away and letting go. It is death and self-destruction to be selfish.

The law of sacrifice is the law of God. God who lived in supreme self-sufficiency as the Father, Son, and Holy Ghost gave Himself. God's glory was in giving Himself, and so He gave Himself in the creation, in the beauty of the universe, so formed that every possible sort of happiness could come according to its natural law. And then God gave Himself in Jesus Christ. "God so loved the world that he gave." He gave His best, gave His all, gave His only begotten Son. The law of God is sacrifice. He loved until He gave ALL.

Then it is the law of Christ Himself. He came through God's sacrifice, and He came to sacrifice. He laid His honors down, left the society of heaven for a generation, and lived with creatures farther beneath Him than the groveling earthworm is beneath a man. He made Himself one of them, and became a brother of this fallen race. He was always yielding and letting go, always holding back His power and not using it. He was always being subject to the will of the men beneath Him, until at last they nailed Him to the cross. His whole life was a continual refusing of Himself, carrying their burdens and sharing their sorrows. And so love and sacrifice is the law of Christ. "Bear ye one another's burdens, and so fulfill the law of Christ." The law of Christ is the bearing of others' burdens, the sharing of others' griefs, sacrificing yourself for another.

It is the law of Christianity. It is the law of the saint. It is the only way to be saved. From the beginning it has always been so. It was so on Mt. Moriah where Abraham, the father of the faithful, gave up his only child, the child of promise. It reached its climax on Mt. Calvary. All along, the way was marked by blood and sacrifice. Not only did Abraham give up his Isaac, but Isaac gave up his life and all through his life he laid himself down for others. We know how Jacob served for his wife, and then did not get the one of his choice. His was a suffering life, a passive life, a patient life. And so Joseph died to his circumstances. Because he was to rise so high, he must go down as low; down not only into banishment but into shameful imprisonment and almost into death. When Joseph was out of sight and all God's promises concerning him seemed lost, and his prospects seemed hopeless, then God picked him up and set him on the world's throne.

Moses had to be a fugitive. Moses had to try and then fail and for forty years God had to teach him and train him, and when at last Moses was out of sight, He gave him his desire. At the very last moment Moses had to let go the prospect of entering the Promised Land. He died outside the gates of Canaan, sacrificed his most cherished hope and waited until the years should roll by and Jesus Himself should bring him in to stand with Him on the Mount of Transfiguration and say, "Now, Moses, you have the thing you let go, the thing you lost and died to; now you have a better resurrection." And so it was all through the past. Saul would not give up himself, would not destroy

Agag and Amalek, types of the flesh. So Saul, head and shoulders above the people, all that a man could be, went down into the darkness, sank into obscurity and shame and perhaps perdition. There was Jonah, the man whom God honored to deliver His own people and lead His kingdom into victory and mighty power in the days of Jeroboam II, the man whom God honored to be the first foreign missionary, the man whom god picked up and sent to Assyria, and said, "Go and preach to Nineveh, go bring the world to know and honor Me." God mightily blessed him. He blessed so mightily that in that city the mightiest revival the world ever saw was consummated. Yet Jonah got angry because God did not kill all the people in Nineveh, and so compromised Jonah's reputation. Jonah had said that the people should die in forty days, but before the forty days were up the people repented of their sins and God repented of what He said and forgave them, and Jonah said, "Where am I in this transaction? I will never be believed again. Why did you not destroy Nineveh and save my reputation? And because Jonah could not let his own glory go, God had to dishonor him and leave him under the withered gourd, a sort of scarecrow to show to all generations how contemptible it is to seek one's own glory. I think there is no more shocking and ridiculous spectacle than that poor old prophet sitting under his withered gourd scolding God and begging to die just because God had dishonored him in fulfilling his mission in the repentance of the whole nation. And God just let him stand there as a spectacle of the shame and dishonor of selfishness.

The New Testament gives the story of Simon Peter's experience. The Master's last message to him when He restored him was: "When thou wast young thou girdedst thyself and walkedst whither thou wouldest; but when thou shalt be old, thou shalt stretch forth thy hands and another shall gird thee and carry thee whither thou wouldest not." This spake He, signifying by what death he should glorify God. And Jesus sent him to a life of crucifixion to be yielded, submissive, surrendered and led about by others against his natural choice till at last he should be crucified with downward head upon his Master's cross.

The world says, look out for yourself; but Jesus says, "Not I, but Christ." Not only must the old self be crucified but the new man with all his strength and self-confidence, too, must die. Not only Ishmael must go out and be an outcast, but Isaac must be yielded and not hold up his head again.

It is so easy to talk about this. The longer I live, the longer I know myself and friends, the more thoroughly I am satisfied that this is the secret of failure among Christians. Too many come a little way with Jesus but stop at Gethsemane and Calvary. They follow him in His ministry in Galilee. The Sermon on the Mount was splendid morality. They loved the feeding of the thousands, and said, "What a blessed king he would make!" They would not have to work as they used to. But when He stood and talked about Calvary and the cross for them as well as for Himself, and how they must go with Him and go with Him all the way, they say, "This is a hard saying, who can bear it?"

A few days later they said, "We do not understand Him; we thought He would be a king." They were not willing to go to the cross.

This is where multitudes have stopped short. They have said yes to self and no to God, instead of saying no to self and yes to God. It is so much easier to talk of this truth than to live it. There is no use to talk about it unless the Holy Ghost shall bring it home to us. A writer once said that there are three baptisms to be baptized with. First, the baptism of repentance, when we turned from sin to God. Second, the baptism of the Holy Ghost, when we receive the Holy Ghost to live in us. Third, the baptism into death, after the Holy Spirit comes in. While he perhaps has no scriptural authority for this precise distinction, there is no doubt that there are these three steps to take. After one receives the baptism of the Holy Ghost, after God comes to live in him, after the Holy Spirit makes the heart His home, then it is that he has to go with Christ into His own dying, and so He says, "If any man will come after me, let him deny himself and take up his cross daily and follow me." And so He said about Himself, "I have a baptism to be baptized with, and how am I strengthened until it be accomplished." I have a burial to be buried with. He was going out into deeper dying every day, and His heart was all pent up with it, until He went down into Gethsemane, down to Joseph's tomb, and down into Hades; and He passed through the regions of the dead and opened first the gates of heaven. That is what Jesus saw before Him after He was baptized on the banks of Jordan.

O beloved, who have received the baptism of the Holy Ghost, it is you who have to go down into His death. Now, I know that in a sense we took all that by faith when we consecrated ourselves to Christ, and we count it all real and God counts it all real; but, my dear friends, we have to go through it step by step. I know God treats the believer as though it was accomplished, as though he were sitting yonder on the throne. But he must go through the narrow passage and the secret places of the stairs. There must be no fooling here. One may count it all done; but step by step it must be written on the records of the heart.

Now, my friends, what does all this mean? It is dying to self-will. After complete consecration to God there often comes a tug of war. The next morning the believer will have the most awful battle of his life. Just because he has given up his will, the devil wants him to take it back. Do not think it will be an Elysian field; no, it will be a battlefield; battles with the dragon and the fiery darts. The devil will try to show how unreasonable consecration is, how right it is that one stand for his own will. It will be life or death perhaps for a week or for a month. Jesus went into the wilderness for forty days, and the devil tried to have Him have His own will, but He stood the test. He let His own will go, "I came not to do mine own will, but the will of him that sent me."

God could make Him a leader because He had been led. No man can govern until he has been governed. Joseph could not have been where he was in Egypt unless he had been set upon by the people and then he sat there a broken man and a lowly, humble spirit. His brothers came down to see him. The world would have said, "Make them feel how mean they were and how wicked." God said, "No, help them to forget it"; and so Joseph said, "Don't be angry or grieved with yourselves, God meant it for good." If Joseph had not been humbled, he would have been no good as Egypt's ruler. No man can lead until he has been led. David had to have nine years of training, and it might have been better for him to have had nine more, then he would not have abused so shamefully his power when he got to the throne. Daniel in

Babylon had to be disciplined by suffering before he could sit as Premier with Cyrus and Nebuchadnezzar. If God is going to make anything of you, let all your will go into His hands. You will find a good many tests after the first surrender, but these are just opportunities for allowing the work to be done.

Then comes self-indulgence, doing a thing because we like to do it. No man has a right to do a thing for the pleasure it affords, because he enjoys or likes it. I have no right to take my dinner just because I like it. This makes me a beast. I do it because it nourishes me. Doing things just because they please us is self-seeking and wrong. "Seek ye first the kingdom of God and His righteousness." We have no divine warrant to seek ourselves in anything. Seek God, and God will seek your good. Take care of the things of God, because He will take care of you. Look not every man on his own things, but on the things of others.

There is self-complacency, dwelling on the work that one has done. How easy after performing some service or gaining some victory to think "How good." How quickly this runs into vain glory! How many are more interested in what people think and say of them than what they are themselves.

In the work of God there is nothing we need to so guard against as vanity. That was Jonah's curse. The seraphim covered their faces with their wings, they covered their feet with their wings. They covered their faces because they did not want to see their beauty, and their feet because they did not want to see their service, nor have anyone else see them. They used only two wings to fly. Take care how you put temptation in another's way. It is all right to encourage workers with a

"God bless you." But don't praise. God does not say, "How beautiful, how eloquent, how lovely, how splendid!" That is putting on a human head the crown that belongs to Jesus. I want the Holy Ghost to enable me simply to do you good, but I do not want power to bring me the honor of the world. If I had it, I should feel it the greatest peril of my life. We have no more right to take Christ's honors here than we have to sit on Jesus' throne and let angels worship us. We have to be so careful when God uses us to bless human souls. There is a sweetness which is not of God. God save us from all these snares woven by the tempter.

Philip, as soon as he had led the eunuch to Jesus, got out of the eunuch's way. Beloved, there are subtle attachments that come between man and man, between woman and woman, and between man and woman. They seem sweet and right, but you need much of the Holy Ghost to keep your spirit pure. I am not talking here of sinful love. Surely, it is not needful to speak of that. I am thinking of far more subtle and refined attractions which are more dishonoring to God and more dangerous, because they are so pure. God keep us from every service, and every friendship, and every thought that is not in the Holy Ghost and not to the honor of Jesus alone.

Then there is self-confidence, that feels its strength, spiritual or mental self-righteousness, power to be good or do good. God has to lead us to lay all that aside and realize our utter nothingness.

God is not pleased with the sensitiveness of the self-life, that fine susceptibility of the feelings that are easily wounded, or that selfish desire one may have to be loved because one seeks affection. Divine love loves that it may bless and do good.

We ought to love, not because it pleases us, but because it blesses others. Paul could say, "...I will very gladly spend and be spent for you; though the more abundantly I love you, the less I be loved" (II Cor. 12:15). He does not say, I will help you as long as you love me. No; I gladly spend my last drop of blood to bless you even when I know you don't appreciate me the least bit. That is what is the matter with you. People hurt you, they don't appreciate you. Well, spend and be spent all the more when you are the less loved.

Time would fail to tell of selfish desires, covetousness, selfish motives, and selfish possession, that give the believer loads of trouble, and worry, just because he insists on owning them.

There are selfish sorrows. I know of nothing more selfish than the tears we shed for our own sorrows. When God saw Israel weeping he was angry and said, "You have polluted my altar with your tears." You are weeping because you have not better bread. You are weeping because something else is dearer to you than Christ. You are weeping because you are not altogether pleased or gratified.

Our sacrifices and self-denials may be selfish. Yes, even one's claim to sanctification may be selfish. A sarcastic friend said of a person that testified about their sinlessness, "Poor old soul, she committed the biggest sin of her life for she told the biggest lie." Self can get up and pray and sit down and say, "What a lovely prayer." Self can preach a sermon and save souls and go home, pat itself on the back and say, or let the devil say through him, "You did splendidly; what a useful man you are!" Self can be burned to death and be proud of its fortitude. Yes, we can have religious selfishness as well as carnal selfishness.

How can we get rid of this? Only by seeing the danger of sin can victory be maintained. Face the sin frankly and determine that it must go. The worst of it is that it deceives us so. It says, "How that fits somebody else, not me." Many apply the truth to others and do not apply it to their own life. One must pass the sentence of death on it or else it will pass sentence on him. Sin is like the serpent with beautiful spots on it like jewels but has the sting of death in it.

May God expose everything in us that will not stand the searching flames. Let us not have a bigger gospel than we have a life. Having passed sentence of death upon self take Jesus Christ and the Holy Spirit to do the work. Don't try to fight it.

Then when the test comes and God leads us out to meet the test, let us be true. The test will often come in the very area of the self-life where the victory was won. When the battle comes, forget self; don't defend it but say, "Lord, keep me." Perhaps someone will try to provoke us. Perhaps someone will try to praise us. Just say, "Yes, the Lord let you come to see if we wanted to be appreciated." The Holy Spirit is able to take everything we dare to give and gives everything we dare to take. "He is able to keep you from falling and to present you faultless." What a blessed exchange it will be! Take the cross and we shall some day wear the crown, sit upon the throne, and all that he is we shall be, and all that He has we shall share.

RESURRECTED, NOT RAISED

("If ye then be risen with Christ" Col. 3:1).

Resurrected with my risen Saviour,
Seated with Him at His own right hand;

This the glorious message Easter brings
  me.
  This the place in which by faith I stand.

Men would bid you rise to higher levels.
  But they leave you on the human plane.
We must have a heavenly resurrection;
  We must die with Christ and rise again.

Once there lived another man within me,
  Child of earth and slave of Satan he;
But I nailed him to the cross of Jesus,
  And that man is nothing now to me.

Now another man is living in me,
  And I count His blessed life as mine;
I have died with Him to all my own life;
  I have risen to all His life Divine.

Oh, it is so sweet to die with Jesus!
  And by death be free from self and sin.
Oh, it is so sweet to live with Jesus!
  As he lives the death-born life within.

There is a great difference between risen and
resurrected. One may rise from one level to
another; but when one is resurrected he is brought
from nothing into existence, from death to life, and
the transition is simply infinite. A true Christian
is not raised but resurrected. The great objection
to all the teachings of mere natural religion and
human ethics is that they teach us to rise to higher
planes. The glory of the Gospel is that it does not
teach us to rise, but shows our inability to do anything good of ourselves, and lays us at once in the
grave in utter helplessness and nothingness, and
then raises us up into new life, born entirely

from above and sustained alone from heavenly sources.

The Christian life is not self-improving, but it is wholly supernatural and Divine. Now the resurrection cannot come until there has been the death. This is presupposed, and just as real as the death has been will be the measure of the resurrection life and power. Do not fear, therefore, to die and to die to all that should be left behind, and to die to self and really cease to be. We lose nothing by letting go, and we cannot enter in till we come out. If we be dead with Him, we shall also live with Him.

But the passage Colossians 3:1, expresses the fact the believer has already died and risen, and should take the attitude of those for whom this is an accomplished fact. He does not call upon them here to die again with Christ and rise with Him anew, as those who have done it are expected to live on a corresponding plane. He tells them later, in the passage, "For ye have died and your life is hid with Christ in God."

In the sixth chapter of Romans this thought is much more fully worked out. "That as many of us as were baptized unto Jesus Christ," the apostle says, "were baptized into his death." Therefore we are buried with him by baptism into death: that like as Christ was raised from the dead by the glory of the Father, even so we also should walk in newness of life" (Rom. 6:3, 4). To emphasize more forcibly the finality of this fact, he says, "Knowing this, that Christ being raised from the dead dieth no more; death hath no more dominion over him. For in that he died, he died unto sin once: but in that he liveth, he liveth unto God." Therefore, and in like manner, the apostle bids us to "reckon ye also yourselves to be dead indeed unto sin, but alive unto God through Jesus Christ...yield yourselves unto God as those that are alive from the dead, and your members as instruments of righteousness unto God" (Rom. 6:9-11, 13).

Now, much of the teaching of the day would bid us yield ourselves unto God to be crucified and to die afresh, or more fully, but the apostle says nothing of the kind here. On the contrary, we are to yield ourselves unto God as those who have already died and are alive from the dead, recognizing the cross as behind us; and for this very reason presenting ourselves to God, to be used for His service and glory.

Have you never seen a bird soaring in midheaven with its mighty pinions spread upon the bosom of the air and floating in the clear sky without a fluttering feather or apparently the movement of a muscle? It is poised in midair; floating in the sky, far above the earth; it does not need to rise, it has risen and is benefiting from its high altitude. Very different is the movement of the little lark that springs from the ground and, beating its wings in successive efforts mounts up to the same aerial heights to sing its morning song, and then returns again to earth. One is the attitude of rising and the other is the attitude of risen.

How can we reckon ourselves dead when we find so many evidences that we are still alive, and how can we reckon ourselves risen when we find so many things that pull us back again to a lower plane? It is the failure to reckon and abide that drags one back. It is the recognizing of the old life as still alive that makes it real and keeps us from overcoming it. This is the principle which underlies the whole Gospel system, that we receive according to the reckoning of our faith. The magic wand of faith will lay all the ghosts that can rise in the cemetery of the soul; and the spirit of doubt will bring them up from the grave to haunt us as long as we continue to question. The only way we can ever die, is by surrendering ourselves to Christ and reckoning ourselves dead with Him.

It is a portentous fact that spiritualism claims the power to rehabilitate in the forms of flesh and blood the spirits of the dead. It is not an uncommon thing for a deceased father to appear to his child, and even speak to her in the old familiar tone, and tell of things that nobody could know but he, until the credulous mind is compelled to believe it is the same person, and that the buried father is truly alive. But it is not true. It is a lie. He is as dead as when he was laid in the tomb; his body is still there, corrupting in the ground, and his spirit is in the eternal world, although he seems to be alive. What does it mean? It is one of the devil's lies. Satan has impersonated that father. He has supernatural power to paint upon the air the forms of those that have passed away, and to speak from those lips until they seem to be real. This is one of the mysteries and yet realities of the present day, and no wise or well-informed man will attempt to dispute it. But the explanation is this;—It is simply a creation of Satan before our senses to deceive us. What is the remedy? Refuse to recognize it. Reckon it dead. Tell it to its face, it is not the father, but one of the devil's brood, and it will immediately disappear. There is one thing Satan cannot stand and that is to be ignored and slighted. He lives on attention and dies of neglect. So if we will refuse to recognize the manifestation of spiritualism, we will always find that it will disappear and have no power to continue its movements. It is wholly dependent on the consent of the will.

Now, here is a fine illustration of the principle of the Gospel. One surrenders himself to Christ to be crucified with Him, and to have all the old life pass out, and henceforth to live as one born from heaven and animated by Him alone. Suddenly, some of his old traits of evil reappear, old thoughts, evil tendencies assert themselves and say loudly "We are not dead." Now if he recognizes these things, fears them and obeys them, they will control him and drag him back into the former state. But if he refuses to recognize them, and says, "These are Satan's lies, I am dead indeed unto sin; these do not belong unto me, but are the children of the devil, I therefore repudiate them and rise above them," God will detach him from them and make them utterly dead. They were no part of him, but simply temptations which Satan tried to throw over him, and to weave around him that which seemed part of himself.

This is the true remedy for all the workings of temptation and sin. It is an awful fact that when one counts himself wicked he will become wicked. Let that pure girl be but made to believe that she is degraded and lost to virtue, and she will have no heart to be pure. She will recklessly sink to all depths of sin. Let the child of God but begin to doubt his acceptance and expect to look upon his Father's face with a frown, and he will have no heart to be holy, he will sink into disobedience, discouragement, and sin.

There is a strange story written by a gifted mind, describing a man who was two men alternately. When he believed himself to be a noble character, he was noble and true, and lived accordingly; but when the other ideal took possession of him and made him feel degraded, he went down accordingly. "As a man thinketh in his heart, so is he." Our reckonings often reflect themselves in our realities; therefore, God has made this principle of faith to be the mainspring of personal righteousness and holiness, and the subtle, yet sublime, power that can lead men out of themselves into the very life of God.

Beloved, shall we let the Master teach us not so much to rise as to remember we are risen; that we have been raised with Christ from the dead, resurrected from the grave of our nothingness, and worse than nothingness, and that we are sitting with Him in heavenly places, recognized by the Father and permitted to reckon ourselves as being, "even as He."

Our attitude will influence our aim. People live according to their standing. The highborn child of nobility carries in his bearing and his mien the consciousness of his noble descent, and so those who have their title to be on high, and consciousness of their high and heavenly rank, walk as children of the kingdom. The remainder of this chapter is devoted to working out this most practical idea, because to be risen with Christ, is to live accordingly.

The argument against lying is that one must put off the old man and put on the new man. The believer has ceased to be a pauper and has become a prince. Therefore, we are to put off the rags of the beggar and wear the epaulette of the prince. We have put on the new man, therefore, let us put on kindness, humbleness of mind, meekness, long-suffering, and over all that charity, which is a perfect girdle that binds all the garments together. We are to put on Christ Himself, the best of all our robes. This resurrection life is intensely practical. The apostle brings it into touch with the closest relationships of life, with the family circle, with masters and servants, and with all the secular obligations of life. It is to affect our whole conduct and leads us to walk wherever He calls.

This draws attention to the practical power there is in being raised up together with Christ. It has power, in the first place, to confirm our hope and assurance of salvation because the resurrection of Jesus was the finishing work and a guarantee to men and angels that the ransom price was paid and the work of atonement complete. When Jesus came forth triumphant from the tomb, it was evident to the universe that the purpose for which He went there was fulfilled, the work He undertook was satisfactorily done, and the Father was satisfied with His finished atonement. Therefore, faith can rest upon His resurrection, as an everlasting foundation, and say: "Who is he that condemneth? It is Christ that died, yea rather, that is risen again, who is even at the right hand of God, who also maketh intercession for us" (Rom. 8:34).

The resurrection of Christ is the power that sanctifies. It enables us to count our own life, our former self, annihilated, so that we are no longer the same person in the eyes of God, and may with confidence repudiate self, and refuse either to obey or fear our former evil nature. Indeed, it is the risen Christ Himself who comes to dwell within, and becomes the power of this new life and victorious obedience. It is not merely the fact of the resurrection, but the fellowship of the Risen One that brings victory and power. One has learned the meaning of the sublime paradox, "I have been crucified with Christ. Nevertheless, I live, yet not I, but Christ liveth in me." This is the only true and lasting sanctification, the indwelling life of Christ, the Risen One, in the believing and obedient soul.

There is power in the resurrection to heal us. He that came forth from the tomb on that Easter morning was the physical Christ, and that body of His is the Head of our bodies, and the foundation of physical strength, as well as spiritual life. If we will receive and trust Him, He will do as much for our bodies as for our spirits, and we shall find a new supernatural strength as the power of the future resurrection touches our physical bodies.

Christ's resurrection also energizes faith and encourages the believer to claim answers to prayer, and ask difficult things from God. What can be too difficult or impossible after the open grave and the stone rolled away? God is trying to teach us. . ."the exceeding greatness of his power to us-ward who believe, according to the working of his mighty power, Which he wrought in Christ, when he raised him from the dead, and set him at his own right hand in the heavenly places" (Eph. 1:19, 20). This is the measure that God is able and willing to do in the name of Jesus under a Christian dispensation. Christ's resurrection is a pledge of all we can ask for, and if we fully believed in the power of that resurrection we would take much more than we have ever done.

The resurrection of the Lord Jesus Christ is the power for true service. The testimony of His resurrection is always peculiarly used by the Holy Spirit as the power of God unto the salvation of men. It was the chief theme of the ministry of the early apostles. They were always preaching of Jesus and the resurrection. It gives a peculiar brightness and attractiveness to Christian life and Christian work. Many Christians look as gloomy as if they were going to their own funeral. We heard not long ago of a little girl who met some gloomy looking people on the road and she said, "Mother, those are Christians, aren't they?" And when the mother asked her why she thought so, she said, "They look so unhappy."

This is the type of Christianity that comes from the cloister and the cross. This is not the Easter type, and certainly it is not the higher type. The religion of Jesus should be as bright as the blossoms of the spring, the songs of the warbling birds and the springing pulses of reviving nature. Our Lord met the women on that bright morning with the cheering message, "All hail," and so He would meet each one that believes on the morning of his new Christian life and bid him go forth with the joy of the Lord as his strength.

This joy springs from the resurrection and is maintained in the heavenlies by the ascended Lord. This is the message that a sad and sinful world needs today. Its motto must not be the "Ecce homo" of the judgment hall, but the glad "All hail!" of the Easter dawn. The more of the indwelling Christ and the resurrection life there is in Christian work the more will be its power to attract, sanctify, and save the world.

Christ's resurrection enables us to meet the hardest places in life and endure its bitterest trials. Philippians says that the power of His resurrection is to bring us into the fellowship of His sufferings, and make us conformable unto His death. We go into the resurrection life that we may be strong enough to suffer with Him and for Him.

Now, let there be no misunderstanding here. This does not mean personal suffering through sickness or the struggles of the spiritual life. These sufferings ought to belong to the earlier period of our experiences. Christ had no conflicts about His sanctification and no physical disease to contend with during His life. So, in bearing these the believer is not bearing the sufferings of Christ. His sufferings are for others, and the power of His resurrection will bring us to share His high and holy sorrows for His suffering church and a dying world. It is a fact that the harder the place and the lower the sphere of toil and suffering the more the elevation of His grace and glory is needed to meet it. From the heights we must reach the depths. The epistles, which lift us into heavenly places, bring us back in every instance to the most commonplace duties, the most ordinary relationships and the most severe trials. These letters to the Ephesians and the Colossians which speak about the highest altitudes of faith and power, speak also more than any others of the temptations common to men, and the duties of husbands and wives, and the need of truthfulness, sobriety, honesty and righteousness, and all the most unromantic, practical experiences of human life.

There is a very remarkable passage in Isaiah which seems to be parallel with the thought in Philippians. It tells us of those that mount up with wings as eagles; but immediately afterwards we find the same persons coming down to the ordinary walks of life, "to run and not be weary, to walk and not faint." It would seem as if the mounting up was just intended to fit them for the running and walking, and that the higher experiences of grace and glory were just designed to enable them to tread the lower level of toil and trial. It is in keeping with this that the apostle speaks of glorying in tribulation. "Glory" expresses the highest attitude of the soul, and "tribulation" the deepest degree of suffering. It teaches that when we come to the deepest and lowest place we must meet it in the highest and most heavenly spirit. This is coming down from the Mount of Transfiguration to meet the demoniac in the plain below, and cast out the power of Satan from a suffering world. Yes, these are the sufferings of Christ. The power of His resurrection is designed to prepare us, enable us, and help us to rise into all the heights of His glorious life, that like Him we may go forth to reflect it in blessing upon the lives of others, and find even sweeter joy in the ministrations of holy love than we have in the ecstasies of the Divine communion.

8

Union with Christ

"For both he that sanctifieth and they that are sanctified are all of one; for which cause he is not ashamed to call them brethren" (Heb. 2:11).

This whole passage is a beautiful picture of our identification with Christ. We are

One with Him in Nature.

"Forasmuch then as the children are partakers of flesh and blood, He also himself likewise took part of the same" (Heb. 2:14a), "For verily, he took not upon him the nature of angels, but he took upon him the seed of Abraham" (Heb. 2:16). How precious this word "likewise!" He has the very same humanity with man and by actual sympathy understands every instinct, feeling, hope, and fear. Not only has He a human body, but a reasonable soul and all the attributes of mind, and all the sensibilities of heart which we possess, and not only so, He still retains this perfect humanity. He has carried it to the right hand of God.

    Partaker of the human name,
    He knows the frailty of our frame.

Let not the transcendent glory of His Deity obscure this glorious important truth. He who is the Son of God is equally the Son of Man. But next,

He is also

One in Sonship,

"for which cause He is not ashamed to call them brethren." "Behold I and the children whom God hath given me." Not only does He come down into humanity, but He also takes the saints up into His Divinity; for they are, indeed, through Him, "partakers of the Divine nature." His own very being is imparted to the believer and he shares His actual relation to the Father. "Go tell my brethren," He says to Mary, "that I go to my Father and your Father, to my God and to your God." It is not that we are adopted into sonship, as a poor child of obscure birth may be received into a noble family, to become the legalized son and heir, but it is as if that child could be reborn into the very blood of that highborn house. We have been actually made partakers of the same nature as God. Hence the Apostle John has finely expressed the deep reality of our sonship in his wonderful words, "Behold what manner of love the Father hath bestowed upon us that we should be called the sons of God"; and then he adds, "and we are the sons of God," not merely called and even legally declared the sons of God, but actually the sons of God by receiving the life and nature of God, and therefore the brethren of our Lord; not only in His human nature, but still more in His Divine relationship. "Therefore He is not ashamed to call us brethren." He gives us that which entitles us to that right and makes us worthy of it. He does not introduce us into a position for which we are uneducated and unfitted, but He gives us a nature worthy of our glorious standing; and as He shall look upon us in our complete and glorious exaltation, reflecting His own likeness and shining in His Father's glory, He shall have no cause to be ashamed of us.

Even now He is pleased to acknowledge us before the universe and call us brethren in the sight of all earth and heaven. Oh, how this dignifies the humblest saint of God! How little we need mind the misunderstandings of the world if He "is not ashamed to call us brethren!" It is said that an English officer was once being treated with neglect and scorn by his fellow officers on account of his promotion from an obscure position to higher rank. They were not willing to forget his humble birth, and passed him by with neglect and coldness. His commanding officer heard of it and so one day he stepped into his tent and talked to him for some time, and then taking him by the arm, the two of them walked for half an hour in front of the other officers' tents. The officers saluted their commanding officer as he passed them, in profound respect, in which his companion shared. He then left the ground, while they looked after him in amazement and humiliation, and after that day there was no lack of respect for the new officer. His commander was not ashamed to own him.

Thus our blessed Brother claims kinship with the believer before earth and heaven; thus He presents his prayers before the throne and owns his name before His Father's face, and makes the name of a mortal to be honored in the highest court in this universe.

One in Spiritual Experience

But again, He is one with us in spiritual experience. The same grace which we receive He also had to receive; the same faith which we have to exercise, He exercised. In this passage, He speaks of putting His trust in God, just as we trust, and praising Him for deliverance in the midst of the church just as we do when we receive our blessings. The Great Forerunner has already passed over the pathway of the Christian life, so wherever the sheep follow He has gone before.

This wonderful truth is sometimes difficult to realize. Christ is depicted as dropping down from heaven with a life all foreign and sublime, that we do not quite take in without much thought, the full meaning of His teachings, that He, like us, was led through all the discipline of a life of faith and dependence; that He could truly say, "I, my own self can do nothing. As I hear, I speak. I came not to do mine own will, but the will of Him who sent me." "The Son can do nothing of Himself," "As the Father sent me and I live by the Father, so he that eateth me, even he shall live by me." He was dependent on the resources of prayer, communion with God, the constant supply of the Holy Spirit, and He understands all the struggles of spiritual life by actual affinity.

Hence we find Him in the prophetic picture exclaiming, "He is near that justifieth me; who is he that shall contend with me? Therefore have I set my face like a flint, and I know that I shall not be ashamed." This was the language of faith, a faith that overcame in the hour of trial, just as we overcome. Not only had He the same experience as we, but He brings us into His very experience. This is really the nature of true sanctification, that it imparts to us the sanctity of Christ. This is the meaning of the passage: "He that sanctifieth and they who are sanctified are all one." He gives His own sanctity and makes His people one with Him in His spirit of holiness. It was this that He meant when He said, "For their sakes I sanctify myself, that they also may be truly sanctified." He consecrated Himself to live in His people and reproduce His own pure and perfect life in their experience. Holiness is thus the indwelling of the Holy Christ, the unity of a human spirit with the spirit of Jesus.

But again, He is

One with Us in Trial.

"For it became Him for whom are all things, and by whom are all things in bringing many sons to glory, to make the Captain of their salvation perfect through suffering"; "therefore He was in all points tempted like as we are, yet without sin." Therefore He has passed through every variety of human suffering, and is now able, from actual experience, to sympathize with and succor those who are tempted, and to make them realize that they are never alone in their afflictions, but understood by His kindred heart and sustained by His sympathy and love. Not only so, but He still retains this power of sympathy and feels the throb of our every pain, for He is able to be "touched with the feeling of our infirmities." The word "touched" expresses a great deal. It means that our troubles are His troubles, and that in all our afflictions He is afflicted. It is not a sympathy of sentiment but a sympathy of suffering.

There is much help in this for the tired heart. It is the foundation of His Priesthood, and God meant that it should be to us a source of unceasing consolation. Let us realize, more fully, our oneness with our Great High Priest, and cast all our burdens on His great heart of suffering love. If we know what it is to ache in every nerve with the responsive pain of our suffering child, we can form some idea how our sorrows touch His heart, and thrill His exalted frame. As the mother feels her baby's pain, as the heart of friendship echoes every cry from another's woe, so in heaven, our exalted Savior, even amid the raptures of that happy world, suffers with all His children bear. "Seeing then that we have a great high priest...Let us therefore come boldly unto the throne of grace" (Heb. 4:14a, 16a). Let us bear with patience the yoke as He carries the heavier end. But He is also

One with the Believer in Death.

Not only does He suffer all the trials of His lot but He is not exempt from mortal fate; for we read that God appointed that He through the grace of God should taste death for every man, ". . .that through death He might destroy him that had the power of death, that is, the devil; And deliver them who through fear of death were all their lifetime subject to bondage" (Heb. 2:14, 15). Even the dark gates of this last prison house He too has entered. There is something very suggestive in the expression that "He should taste death for every man." It seems to suggest that He had all the bitterness of the cup to drain and has taken the taste out of death for all who are united with Him. There is no poison in the cup now and no virulence in the sting. He tasted it; but the bitterness of death is past if we are in Him. "For if a man keep my sayings he shall never see death." He shall only see the face of our blessed Lord and the open gates of heaven. All the death that was in the cup, Christ has drunk, and there is the glad shout, "Thanks be to God, which giveth us the victory through our Lord Jesus Christ" (I Cor. 15:57).

> Death and the curse were in the cup;
> Oh, Christ, 'twas full for Thee!
> But Thou hast drained the last dark drop,
> 'Tis empty now for me.
> For me, Lord Jesus, Thou hast died,
> And I have died in Thee;
> Thou'rt risen, my bands are all untied,
> And now Thou livest in Me.

Finally, He is

One with Us in Glorious Destiny.

The writer of the Book of Hebrews quotes from the eighth Psalm, which describes the future dignity and destiny of man. The psalmist speaks of the glorious dignity of man in these words, ". . .thou hast put all things [in subjection] under his feet" (Ps. 8:6b), and the apostle argues if this be literally true, it implies a dignity that leaves nothing that is not put under man, but he says as a matter of actual observation, "But now we see not yet all things put under him" (Heb. 2:8b). How then can the words be true of man? The glorious explanation is that they are true of the Son of Man, the Great Head of the race. "We see not yet all things put under man. But we see Jesus. . .crowned with glory and honor" (Heb. 2:8b, 9a). He takes up the honor of the race and wins the crown of dominion for humanity, and then He shares it all with us. For all that He has won He has won as a man, for redeemed humanity; and has raised us up with Him to sit in heavenly places, that in the ages to come He might show the exceeding riches of His grace in His kindness to us by Christ Jesus. Every crown He wears He shall share with us. "He that overcometh shall sit on His throne, even as He overcame and is set down with His Father on His throne." This is the high and glorious hope of every child of God. This is the meaning of our union with the Son of God. Well may the apostle say, "It doth not yet appear what we shall be: [as the sons of God] but we know that, when he shall appear, we shall be like him; for we shall see him as he is" (I John 3:2). Such a hope may well inspire and unspeakably encourage the children of God.

Let us think of some of its practical applications: first, let us learn the secret even of our faith. It is the faith of Christ, springing in our heart and trusting in our trials. So shall we also sing. "The life that I now live, I live by the faith of the Son of God, who loved me and gave Himself for me." Thus looking off, unto Jesus, "The Author and Finisher of our faith," we shall find that instead of struggling to reach the promises of God, we shall lie down upon them in blessed repose and be borne up by them with the faith which is no more our own than the promises upon which it rests. Each new need will find us leaning afresh on Him for the grace to trust and to overcome.

The true spirit of prayer is the spirit of Christ in us. "In the midst of the church will I sing praises unto thee." Christ still sings these praises in the trusting heart and lifts his prayers into songs of victory. Paul and Silas knew the true spirit of prayer in the prison of Philippi and turned prayer into praise, night into day, the sorrow into joy. When He indwells as the spirit of faith, He will also become the spirit of praise.

But again, this should comfort us in trial; our Brother is bearing all that we bear, and if He can stand it, surely we can. His Father would not allow His own beloved Son to have a needless pain, and therefore we may be sure that there is a "need be" for all we are called to bear. If Christ is carrying the other end of the yoke, we may know it is right and that we shall not sink under the load. Let us then rejoice that we are partakers of the sufferings of Christ that "when His glory shall be revealed we shall be glad also with exceeding joy."

Let this comfort us amid imperfect experiences and realizations of victory. "We see not yet all things put under Him." How true this is to us all! How many things there are that seem to be stronger than we are; but blessed be His name! they are all in subjection under Him, and we see Jesus crowned above them all, and Jesus is our Head, our representative, our other self, and where He is, we shall surely be. Therefore when we fail to see anything that God has promised, and that we have claimed in our experience, let us look up and see it realized in Him, and claim it in Him for ourselves. Our side is only half the circle, the heaven side is already complete, and the rainbow of which we see not the upper half, shall one day be all around the throne and take in the other hemisphere of our now unfinished life. By faith, then, let us enter into all our inheritance. Let us lift up our eyes to the north and to the south, to the east and to the west, and hear Him say, "All the land that thou seest will I give them." Let us remember that the circle is complete, that the inheritance is unlimited, and that all things are put under His feet. Have we counted this true without abatement, or have we discounted it and lost its fullness? Shall we not henceforth "Crown Him Lord of all," and put all things under His feet, and then, keeping step with Him, put our feet on the difficulties and adversaries that we have feared so long, and go out henceforth in the chariot of His Ascension, to sing as we ascend, "Now thanks be unto God, which always causes us to triumph in Christ, and maketh manifest the savor of his knowledge by us in every place" (II Cor. 2:14).